All The Things You Could Be

You Could Be

Written & Illustrated by
Leanne Pastor

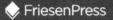 FriesenPress

Suite 300 - 990 Fort St
Victoria, BC, V8V 3K2
Canada

www.friesenpress.com

ISBN
978-1-5255-5192-5 (Hardcover)
978-1-5255-5193-2 (Paperback)
978-1-5255-5194-9 (eBook)

1. JUVENILE NONFICTION, CAREERS

Distributed to the trade by The Ingram Book Company

To all my friends and family who helped this book come to life . . .

Thank-you!

To **YOU,** the dreamer and creator of all the things you could be . . .

Keep following your joy!

To my husband B.J.,
I'm so grateful for your unconditional love and support with this book and always, And that I get to share & create each day with you.

To my daughters Bailee & Harper,
Thank you for inspiring me to create this book & for contributing to this book. Thank you for being YOU! May you always follow your JOY! I'm so grateful for each of you. xoxo

You could be an astronaut,
And fly to the moon.

You could be a musician,
And come up with a tune.

You could be a teacher,
Making lessons and plans.

You could be a traveller,
Discovering new lands.

You could be an artist,
Painting rainbows and trees.

You could be a beekeeper,
Watching over the bees.

You could be a doctor,
Saving lives every day.

You could be an athlete,
Where sports are your play.

Yes,
All of these things you could be
and could do . . .
I wonder, though,

What if you chose to be **YOU?** ,
And what if these things you
already are . . .

Like the astronaut,

BRAVE . . .

You're sure to go far.

Like the musician,

EXPRESSIVE . . .

You speak your mind.

Like the teacher,
ENCOURAGING, PATIENT,
and KIND.

Like the traveller,

EXPLORING

is what you love to do.

Like the artist,

You're always CREATING

things new.

Like the beekeeper,

OBSERVANT

in so many ways . . .
You see the beauty in nature,
And you're not afraid.

Like the doctor,
You're

CARING and KNOW

what to do.

Like the athlete,

DETERMINATION

and

STRENGTH

is in you.

So, if you're unsure
what to be and to do,
Just know that the answers
are all within you.
Follow your joy . . .
What comes easy to you?
Just keep doing that,
And keep being

YOU!

To find this book on the web,
Checkout...

www.allthethingsyoucouldbe.com

For more info about the amazing pho-
tographer who photographed Leanne's
illustrations,

Checkout...
**https://photosnap.ca/region/edmon-
ton-area lee-anne-egan-photography**

About the Author

Leanne Pastor is a Canadian artist and energy healer. She worked as a registered nurse for twelve years, which gave her an appreciation for the precious gift of life. While on maternity leave with her second daughter, she decided to follow her heart and begin a new career path. She became certified in various energy healing modalities, and now enjoys helping others along their own healing journeys. She also rediscovered her lifelong passion for art, and actively enjoys writing and painting. "All the Things You Could Be" is her first book, and she hopes it will inspire children (and adults) to choose what brings them joy and be true to themselves. She currently lives in Sherwood Park, Alberta, with her husband, B. J., and their daughters, Bailee and Harper. In her free time, Leanne enjoys spending time with family and friends, being outdoors, making art, and doing more of what brings her joy each day.

Be Kind Be Brave Be You

CPSIA information can be obtained
at www.ICGtesting.com
Printed in the USA
LVHW070840231119
638233LV00002B/2/P